Praise for

Rosemary Daniell is a national treasure.

—Bruce Feiler, *New York Times*-bestselling author of
The Council of Dads and *Life Is in the Transitions*

Rosemary Daniell is an enormously gifted poet, novelist and
non-fiction writer who has created an extraordinary body of
work over the over the last two decades. Her work is risky—in
the best sense of the term. She brings a poet's language to
her prose and great energy and daring to her poetry. She is
one of the women by whom our age will be known in times
to come. I can think of few writers I might recommend more
whole-heartedly.

—Erica Jong, author of *Fear of Flying*

The world of poetry has just about recovered from the shock
of a woman poet giving us A Sexual Tour of the Deep South
in 1975. As a witness to the prolonged impact of Rosemary
Daniell's first, unique collection, I am astonished to be
unprepared for the shock of reading The Murderous Sky....
Daniell's new collection proves that the critic Warren Austin...
was right when he wrote, "Art makes that beautiful which in
life would be painful to view or even hear about.:

—David Madden, author of *Marble Goddesses and
Mortal Flesh*

In this searing journey through a mother's broken heart,
Rosemary Daniell's exquisitely wrought poems transmute
suffering into splendor, unspeakable pain into echoing beauty,
heralding redemption for both writer and readers.

—Joyce Zonana, author of *Dream Homes: From Cairo
to Katrina, an Exile's Journey*

Rosemary Daniell is a supreme storyteller. Exploring the ordinary in verse, she makes it belong to us all. Taking up the rare with vivid metaphor…. Daniell digs deep into subjects like suicide, drug addiction and abuse—but also love and tenderness. Read her!

—**Linda Gray Sexton**, author of *Searching for Mercy Street: My Journey Back to My Mother, Anne Sexton*

It's hard to say what makes Rosemary Daniell's poetry ring so true, but it is certainly southern, totally honest, and empathic and it always has the right pitch. Whether she is laying bare the immense pain of her own daughter's addiction, her son's schizophrenia or of an idealist gone wrong, she is able to confront that pain and through words begin a process of healing that takes place in the reader's own heart. Thus it is a kind of miracle…. It took courage to write these poems, and it takes courage to read them.

—**Gordon Walmsley**, editor of *The Copenhagen Review* and author of *Braille of the Sea* and other books

If the aura of poetry is colored from the poet's palette of experience and observation, then The Murderous Sky, should be on display in galleries as well as in bookstores. It is that engaging, that powerful, and, yes, that visual…. It begins with these words: "I had a daughter once—/beautiful & raven-haired…", and what follows reads like a poetic excerpt from a revealing memoir, words of privacy that might be whispered in confessionals…. Indeed, this is a signature work from a writer of rare and beautiful talent. Only a true artist is so blessed and her name is Rosemary Daniell.

—**Terry Kay**, author of *Dance with the White Dog* and *The Book of Marie*

The poems in Rosemary Daniell's new book are beautiful and heartbreaking beyond any ordinary exclamation of words. She manages to find the perfect balance between sharing her experiences as the insider looking outward and the outsider looking inward, building a bridge between feeling and form in towering, gut-wrenching language. This is what poetry is meant to do, and The Murderous Sky: Poems of Madness & Mercy is what it looks like to do it well.

—**Olivia Stiffler,** author of *Hiding in Plain Sight* and *Otherwise, We Are Safe*

To read Rosemary Daniell's poetry is to see the power of love do good and do harm. Yes, it is love that flows through these pages, like blood—the love between a mother and daughter, the love between a mother and son. While we're reading poems that show us 'how dangerous life is,' we're also witnessing sacred things: "a few yellow buds… this suddenly is enough." Rosemary Daniell is the real thing. I marvel at the skill and imagination and honesty behind these stunning poems. I just cannot overpraise this book.

—**Judy Goldman**, author of *Together: A Memoir of a Marriage and a Medical Mishap*

These are not poems for the faint-hearted…. *The Murderous Sky* is power-filled, naked and excellent beyond words.

—**Carol Ann Russell**, author of *The Red Envelope, Silver Dollar* and *Gypsy Taxi*

Amid the endless outpourings about the pains of love, how many deal with the love of a mother for her children? What happens when her dreams grow into realities too terrible to be believed or comprehended? Rosemary Daniell, with deep compassion for both sides, takes us into the world of parents and children struggling with drug addiction and mental illness. Like the Book of Job, this book has the courage to face realities larger and far less comfortable than we would like. But it also shows the power of true art to help us survive and transcend.

—**Dan Veach**, founder of *The Atlanta Review* and author of *Elephant Water* and *Lunchboxes*.

This moving and tumultuous collection of poetry scales the mountains of emotion bound up in motherhood and mental illness. Rosemary manages to tell us the story of her daughter and her son, their lineage, and the battles she's fought, with lyric beauty and raw emotion. The reader will come away from this book with a deeper understanding of the ties that bind and tangle mother and child.

—**Miriam Feldman**, author of *He Came in with It: A Portrait of Motherhood and Madness*

The Murderous Sky

Poems of Madness & Mercy

Rosemary Daniell

Lavender Ink
lavenderink.org

The Murderous Sky
Rosemary Daniell

Copyright © 2020 by the author and Lavender Ink,
an imprint of Diálogos Books.

Printed in the U.S.A.
First Printing
10 9 8 7 6 5 4 3 2 1   18 19 20 21 22 23

Book design: Bill Lavender
Cover art: *Le ciel meurtrier (The Murderous Sky)*, by René Magritte. 1927.
Photo: Jacques Faujour. © ARS, Musee National d'Art Moderne, Centre Georges
Pompidou, Paris, France © CNAC/MNAM/Dist. RMN-Grand Palais / Art Resource.
Used by permission.

Library of Congress Control Number: 2020931751
Daniell, Rosemary
The Murderous Sky / Rosemary Daniell
p. cm.
ISBN: 978-1-944884-74-1 (pbk.)

Lavender Ink
lavenderink.org

Other Books By Rosemary Daniell

Secrets of the Zona Rosa

Confessions of a (Female) Chauvinist

The Woman Who Spilled Words All Over Herself

The Hurricane Season

Fort Bragg & Other Points South

Sleeping with Soldiers: In Search of the Macho Man

Fatal Flowers: On Sin, Sex, and Suicide in the Deep South

A Sexual Tour of the Deep South

Acknowledgments

"What Keith the Hunter Said About the Deer in the Hills" and "Of Jesus, Eyes Blazing," appeared in *Arts & Letters*. "Values, or The Christ of the White Shag Carpet" was published in *American Voice*. "Intimate Terrorists" was published in *Kalliope* and was nominated for a Pushcart Prize. "Accommodations" and "The Power of Love" appeared in *The Chattahoochee Review*. "The Murderous Sky" was published in *Poets, Artists & Madmen,* where it won an annual award. "Portrait: Boy with Dog" appeared in *Explicit Lyrics*. "Sacred Things" won the Gold Medal and First Prize in the William Wisdom–William Faulkner Poetry Competition sponsored by the Faulkner Society. "Intimate Terrorists," "Isn't It Ironic," "Luck," "Out West, Where I Took My Grief" (in another form), "The Power of Love," "Values, or the Christ of the White Shag Carpet," "How Dumb Can You Be?", "Daytona Raceway," "The Murderous Sky," "Beautiful Things" and "Wyoming" were also published in an online chapbook on Web del Sol.

Contents

Part One
Pain for a Daughter

Part Two
Without a Mother's Love

Part Three
Beautiful Things

The Murderous Sky

after a painting by René Magritte

For my grandmother Lee, who like me, had a bipolar
daughter and a schizophrenic son.

"Oh, what a power is motherhood, possessing a
potent spell. All women alike fight fiercely for a
child." —Euripides

*And God said: you will not have ordinary happiness.
But you will have this.*

Part One

Pain for a Daughter

"And our prayers were a loud cry to God." —the grandmother of a woman rescued after disappearing during a bout of amnesia

"Where a child would have believed Mama! she bit the towel and called on God… and I saw her, at that moment, in her own death, and I knew that she knew." —Anne Sexton

---

Ancient History

I had a daughter once—
beautiful & raven-haired.
I dreamed her before she was born
her jet curls   her dimples
her face as fair as pearl.
And named her from botany—
"Lily… the pure," the book read.
But even in the hospital
some dark shadow cast
across the page as I lay reading
Love or Perish. "Why so
serious?" the nun asked.
And why *was* I afraid—
that I would drop my newborn
from the high bed   that
the window would fly open
I would jump to my death?
Why during the birth
had I imagined myself
Catherine in *Farewell to Arms*
dying as my blood seeped?
Yet I   at twenty-three   already
the mother of two   could only
save myself by a vision
of floating aloft on a cloud
in the arms of Jesus…

What did I not know then?
What do I know now?
Only how this girl-child
already holding in her heart
the seeds of some ancient grief
would become this woman
sodden & raging   taken
in handcuffs   the small blue stars
of needle tracks at elbow
ankle & wrist. And wonder
if something was telling me:
let the baby drop   save her
drop the baby   save yourself.

Love, Like a Poultice

All night   I hold you in the double bed --
your heat raised to a bird's pitch   your bones
that thin & bunched. As you twist
your teeth shake   sweat drenches the sheets. . .

And if the squirrel can find the acorn
the bird the worm   why can not the good earth
provide what you need   my daughter   even unto
the seed of the poppy   even unto heroin?

The No

One grandmother   after a lifetime
of tears   a suicide (pills)   the other
who killed a child with her Cadillac
drank Drano   burned down a hotel . . .
And then   the grandfather with wet brain
the other   the architect   drowned in booze . . .
So why do we wonder at your tongue
stumbling at *No*   a word in a language
as foreign to you as gibberish   that *No*
that could save your one beautiful life?

Freak

"You cut their legs off when you do that…"
Two words that sound so much alike:
disabled   enabling: which is she
referring to? The dismemberment
of frogs? Chickens? Or my getting you
out of jail   accepting the collect calls
from street corners   telephone booths
making sure you have food to eat
or the desperate one to stay the razor
blade *this* time… And as the words balloon
from her lips   I see it: that photo
of the boy born limbless   his torso
flush to the desert sands.   Is this what
it has come to? Have I through the power
of my love   left you this helpless   this hacked?

Veal

"If you can imagine a banquet table filled with food, and the desire of the starving man standing nearby…" – a doctor, describing the craving of the addict

---

He will be chained by the neck in a tiny wooden crate…
& force-fed a liquid formula… to turn his flesh soft
& pale. He will suffer loneliness, fear, and… distress…
until the butcher's knife ends his agony… reads the card
with the picture of the calf. *Are you really that hungry?*
the text asks.   You   withdrawing from the methadone
say I don't know *what* I would do if I were in your shoes
that if I was in a plane crash in the Andes & was starving
& you   my daughter   were frozen   I would eat even you
my own flesh.   Oh   once   in my arrogance   I begged God
to take *me*   to let *me* go through this.   But now all I know
is that some are destined to such fates   that you   my child
like the calf   like the hungry in Somalia   will starve   while
I   your cries like dinner music or white sound   will eat.

23

Motherhood

for Gladys, who didn't recognize her own son when she saw him in a 7-Eleven

1.

True, the cheetah leaves her
young on the Serengeti
without a backward glance.
Nature lets what will, die.
And no matter how piteously they
cry   huge overgrown children
as big as she   perched on rocks
scanning the vast grasses   or how
they lay sick   unable to feed
themselves: she will not reappear
until a year later   when   from
the distance   they see her   she who once
meant everything   a new set of
cubs at her faithless mother's side.

2.

Why are the sheep shorn
in the cold winds? Because
they won't take their
lambs to safety but
to save their own skins.

3.

And then there is the urge
to kill   like that mother
in the Bronx who shot
her crack-addicted daughter.
Like God & his only son.

Shimmering Salvation

Savannah: June   & already
the asphalt shimmers   as behind me
on the busy street   horns blare:
stop!   a kitten beneath your wheel!
& yes   you tiny thing who lives
in my back yard   with your brother
& sister   hide beneath my bumper
until   before lined-up traffic
I take you   trembling mound of bone
& fluff   a dandelion in dusty
black   into my palm   my lap
thinking   I have saved you.

Then   as I turn the Olds toward home
I see my other would-have-been
stowaway: your sister splayed
on the street   a little ballet dancer
fuzzy limbs crossed in perfect grace…

So I have only saved one of you—
who I return   baring teeth
hissing   racing to your Black
mother's side.   In the house
I dial Vac Com   & shaken
driving again to my errands
see the big white truck   its hose—

flash your sister's body   crushed
whooshed up into that hot tank.

And think how I too once had
three young   yet have only
been able to save one from
that vast suction machine
that huge chemical mouth
that disposal heap of life.

Thwarted Flight

Outside the Embassy Suites   on the sidewalk
on 12th Street   the gray bird   no more than two
inches long   thrashes on her back   like a girl
trying to escape rape: her head jerks from side to side
her creamy breast exposed to those rushing by.
I stop   as does another.   "Poor thing," she murmurs   then
hurries off.   Everything in me wants to walk away   too.
But I have no destination other than the deli
my bagel   egg & cheese.   Animal control   I think
recalling the kitten smashed last June beneath my Olds
& turn toward a phone   hesitate: will that man   his black
wingtips   flatten her?   Or that woman   looking straight
ahead   arm like a piston   pumping her briefcase?   I squat
wrap the fluttering warmth in black silk from my purse
drop her   into its recesses   a strange contraband.
I flash her inside my high rise   the Rack Room shoebox
dying while I watch Jeopardy— how long will that take?
Then   across the street   I see CITY PARK—
under the trees   past the man sleeping   I look
for the right spot for a happy death   or even healing:
not in ivy or wet mulch   nor sun too bright   & find it
beneath a tree   soft grass & twigs.   Turning my purse
I tumble her out   again   feet & feathers flailing
as though she's reluctant to leave its dark depths
her silken mummy's wrap.   With a fingertip   I free
one miniscule claw   as behind me leans a man   brown skin

28

shining within forest twill   Cleveland Public Service
 embroidered yellow on a pocket.   "It must be sick,"
he says   lifting the bird in his palm. "I'll put it
over here in the sun."   I stand freed: he has taken
my hapless patient.   But I recall how the night
 before   from my twelfth-floor window   I saw lightning
striking the dark wet streets   Lake Erie only blocks away
what specks   scurrying below   we are. And how
like this creature I am   thrashing   futilely thrashing.

And at Last, Envy

for Grandmother Lee, whose son and daughter also suffered blows to the chromosomes

---

of those for whom
it is over: of the friend whose mad brother
leaps down the eight floors   of the other
whose father shoots her mother & then himself
leaving her a gift wrapped in red ribbons.
Of the paralyzed woman who   faking
out death   those last dumb moments   drinks herself
into them.   Even of the one in hospice
fading of AIDS   mumbling of China   where
he has not been… Yes   this is the envy
of those for whom the worst has happened:
of the peace with which they sleep while I writhe
trying not to think Panama Beach
the Oxygen Zone Motel where you were
last seen with two men.   Or what the police
said: that if a body is found   what
the fingerprints will reveal…   So once
again   bowels awash   I sit by a phone
as silent as stone: counting syllables
parsing lines   placing words in order
to dam what may come crashing   crashing in.

Faith Healers

are who we turn to
when we can think of no other way—
when the pain is no longer bearable
when the AZT isn't working
when the blood count sinks too low
when the withdrawal starts even
before the junk kicks in.   Everything
alive wants to live   so they say: my
mother   just before her suicide
dreamed of that clinic in Mexico—
my friend started the macrobiotics
the month after the holistic center
the week before he couldn't eat at all.
When they were teenagers   I dreamed
my two daughters: the shy one hurtling
away in a taxi   pressing her face
against the glass   the bold one's body
delivered to my door   draped lifeless
over a trunk.   And now that daughter—

habitué of needles   wrapped
like deadly candies   in cellophane
of sugar daddies & the streets &
razor blades   of candles burning
down at fast forward   tells me
she is Born Again   that it is only
the Spirit that will save her: I toss
in dreams   waiting for the sound—
the thud of the trunk   arriving.

Accommodations

for the man who smokes in Forsyth Park in Savannah, Georgia, each morning

"Behind every work of fiction is an anguished question." —Wallace Stegner

---

The man with the three-part action   first   the arm raised
from his side   the forearm extended   then   the hand lifted
to his lips: the motions as modulated   as predictable
as a mechanical toy made in Germany   has found
his means of accommodation: a perpetual cigarette
between his fingertips. When we pass each morning
near the mental health center   we speak   & he may think
I believe his subterfuge: that he is not required
by the crossed wires of his brain to do this.
But I who have my own obsessive-compulsive disorder
(an obsession with love   a compulsion to save)
 know an accommodation when I see one.

Thirty years ago   my sister   a nurse   told me
of a 17-year-old   dying of cancer: on the day
the girl was told   the high squeal of a rabbit
with its throat cut   rang from the girl's room   spiraled
down the hospital corridor. Within minutes
her mother   came out   into the hallway   admired
the Christmas decorations. As my sister told me this
we   both young mothers   cringed. And yes   there are

those who refuse to accommodate   who faced with the
unbearable   go mad or jump off the sides of buildings.
Then there are the ones who think they can control
tidal waves   the paths of viruses   even change
God's mind.   And when I was younger   I believed
I was one of those: a disturber of the peace
who would scream out her pain   whatever the cost…

But today   I understand that woman better.   Today
I am that woman   watching my own child die
before my eyes   unable to do anything but make
polite conversation.   I too walk down the street
with a vague smile on my face   thinking the kinds
of thoughts people do before searching out faith healers—
still believing that while there's life   there's hope
still praying   like a fool   for some simple crumb.
And does the man with the cigarette know that
while I may not live in the mental health center
while I may know how to shop for shoes in Paris
to dress for a party & make small talk   that I too
am bathed in grief: am as trapped in accommodation
am as reflexive   as struck dumb as he is?

Gangrene

"Man saws off hand, then shoots nails into his head... hoping to end
his pain."—The Associated Press

And then there is the man who
alone in the woods   trapped
beneath the weight of a tree
trunk   cut off his own leg
with a pocket knife   crawled
up a rock-strewn bank   hauled
himself onto his tractor—
with one leg   two hands   drove
to a farm where a man
saw him covered in blood—
"He talked all the way to the
emergency room to keep
from passing out."   And told his
story: "I tried three times
before I could do it" & then
with what violence   what need?
"Pain? What pain?"   he asked
when the nurse offered morphine.
Like me trying to save your life
without knowing my own grief—
how I am rotting from the feet
up   how   you   my love   are my
gangrene.   The leg   it turned out
couldn't be reattached   just

like you can't be whooshed back
inside my womb   safe again.
And can I have the guts he did
to cut off my own   my own flesh?

The Other You

opens the door—
Sunday morning & apricot light
floods the pale space   walls sponged
peach or ecru   canvases stacked like
juicy swatches   your cat   eyes dollops
of Egyptian gold   lolls at an ankle—
you drift in diaphanous cream
"just a thrift shop thing, "you say
your auburn hair a backlit flame.
The rich tones of Italy flicker—
the scent of cinnamon wafts.

We embrace   as we have
a thousand times: I   just off the plane
(from the Islands?   from Mexico?)
your bones slight beneath my fingertips.
And how was the opening last week?
"At least the reviews were good."
Behind you   the man undrapes himself.
But he is incidental. This is about
you and me: I   your mother   aging
you   my daughter   in your prime—
this Other You who is the Other Me
of wet colors   brushstrokes   of mistakes
made yet not grieved.   The You who makes
up for my Southern grandmother's life

the purdah of perfect wife   white gloves
church   for my mother's girlish dreams
of writing   of love, sweet love   gone up
in madness   for the bottles I boiled
the diapers I hung out   the husbands
I escaped   the jobs I took.   The Other You
who is the meaning of the art books
the private schools   the airline tickets
who lives out a freedom I only dreamed.

Yes   this is the You who would have been
before the dark rivers of the lower
Eastside   before the bombed-out buildings
the machine guns overhead   before the sorgham
syrup of heroin through your veins   before
the men with fists like stones   or crude tattoos—
before the years of methadone   sucking out
your marrow   before all this was taken from you
as if by a brush fire or a holocaust…

Oh God   if only I could redirect this film
Oh God   if only I could let parts of it
fall to the cutting room floor   Oh God if
only this was a TV movie   the Other You
running backwards into pure happiness…

Sacred Things

are not
the ancient Chinese tapestry
silk heavy with embroidery
stitched a thousand years ago
that stoned   you cut up
to make an ugly dress.
Or the few pieces of sterling
each stamped with a rose—
left from a wedding before you
were born. Nor was it that
heavy gold snake   my one good
piece of jewelry   coiled
in its box   waiting to be
pawned again. And of course
not that small plastic card
embossed with the magic
numbers with which you carved
the money from my account
as easily as you would
butter with a knife… Or
are they the nights & nights
spent writhing   for though
I   with my sins   am an
unlikely one   turned good
only through default
we know that all mothers

are saints   eager to give,
to give up their own lives…

No   none of these are
the sacred things that stand
like totems   like the cast
Egyptian cat you loved
beside the door to pain as
it heaves   clangs open again.
Nor are these the objets that
lay as though carelessly thrown
onto the stone slab   that
ancient (it seems) rock for
sacrifice   like my heart   gone
blood-stained & blood-stained
born as we were with the black
bile   running in our family
a river (or was it more
like a swamp or quicksand?)…

No. What is   is the snapshot
of you   at three in your red
velvet bowler   the ribbons
bouncing down your plump back—
in your black princess coat with
white fur collar   your fat legs
churning the pedals of your trike—
next   your dimpled arms around

my knees as you beg for red
jam on white bread… Yes, that

& the drawing you made
at eight: your Pitiful Pearl
doll   the tears rolling down
her plastic cheeks   the balloon
over her head reading   MOTHER
PLEASE LOVE ME. Or the sketch
of me at my desk   typing:
"I dreamed the house was on fire
& you wouldn't save me" reads
the caption. And then   captured
by your girlish hand: the water-
color of the hundred-foot pines
the goldfish pond carved of
coral rock   our calico perched
beside it   watching the swerve
of red fish.
                    Or later:

the memory of you   striding
up Fifth Avenue   in high heels
& short fur   gorgeous in
your Italian-boy haircut
(more confident   it seemed
than I had ever been).
And the picture taken by

the famous artist (the one
who was once my lover)
you   newly blonde   a tumble
of gold & cream   trussed in red
velvet for your gig at the
Gaslight Club: a woman
from another century   who
will soon learn the things I—
her mother— will never know
about needles & shooting
galleries   about bombed-out
buildings with men standing
overhead holding guns   about
where one buys the works
neatly cellophaned   & finally
about overdoses   hospitals
& jail cells.

And that was when?
ten years   an eternity   ago?
Before I watched what had been
my vision of you   my beautiful
one   stepping off that Greyhound
eyes purpled by a fist   an old
man's shirt hiding the knife cuts
the blood-black gashes   marking
your perfect flesh   & all your things
(your poor things) stuffed into that

one green plastic garbage bag…

But the most sacred may be
the photo of you   taken five years
ago   your long hair a radiant
shawl to your heart-shaped face
the scars inside your elbows
(like mauve pencil dots) hidden
by the Mary-blue cotton gown
your deep-lashed eyes   shining
with stars (or is it tears?)
into the eyes of your newborn—
Raphael, angel   you called
him. And scrawled on the back
is the fat arrowed heart   tears
dripping from its jagged tear
& inside it   the names of Janie
& Bob   the happy couple   who
the next day   in a lawyer's
staid rooms   will take him from
our arms forever: Oh my
God   my God! cried out the man
I once read of   drawn & quartered
yet still holding in his hands
his own beating heart. And yes
these are the sacred things
the muscle ripped from the
living breast   the wounds made

by blades   rough-edged & blunt
the kinds of sacrifices after
which none ever matters again.

Sleight of Hand

"Human beings can only carry the divine sometimes."—Friedrich Holderlin

"Mother, I have found my mother and I am safe and always have been."—David Ignatow

---

And when you were born   silver glitter fell
from the sky around your still-bloodied head—
never mind that we were really
in Grady Hospital   a kind of
Southern 42nd Street   a building
crawling with the poor   the crazed   the lost.
Or that your mother   my daughter
was a strung-out junkie   cursing
the nurses   the young interns   especially
the one who   because her veins are shot
cut into the side of her neck
the only place the I.V. could enter—
a woman who   in her despair   asked
that her insides be cut   that this
not happen again: that woman who once slid
from me   carrying my love and dreams…
And here you came   a tiny smeared saint
carried by a nurse in your knit cap
eyes clamped shut against a world you didn't
want to see yet.   And we who already
loved you   got up from our hard bench

cheering your triumph at being born
every part intact.   And afterwards
we held you in the nursery
for infants at risk   breathing life   we hoped
into your small face…

               For we dreamed how
in the years to come   every ounce
of your holiness might be called forth
how you too might become   like me: parent
to a mother who remains a child   how
you have been brought to earth to save
everyone but yourself   how the curse
of methadone still coursing your veins
might serve as just the right caustic
the right abrasive sting to teach you
to rise   the glitter falling from your
broad man's shoulders:

               I saw you lifted
high in the streets   above the crowd:
victorious over this caul—
you   a man-child born today
in this public place   raised exultant
through the cut   through the layers of fat
& flesh   the blood let on your behalf
to help you rise   to rise above this…

And Daniel   in your way   perhaps
you have: the way of a babe who slept

through a fog of cigarette smoke
the blue bleat of TV   the hyped-up
junkie talk   the runs for scripts: a babe
who yawned   smiled   clutched a finger
sucked at a bottle   eyes locked
into mine or anyone's   who   fat &
dimpled   slept beside your mother
in her king-sized bed   through her thick sleep
until that moment when you just stopped
(already tired of living   knowing
what was to come?).   And now you lay
in a small grave   the Country of
of the Resurrection: oh   can even
God make sense of the senseless
& what sense will He make of this?   Yet
Daniel   at this moment   you rise
above us all: I see you on your cloud
I feel your immense & innocent
love: drifting down   drifting down…

And as though by sleight of hand   (your small
one passing over   transparent   pink)
will a clean white light come on in your
mother's brain   once more illumining
the fineness with which she too was born?

A Daughter Walks in Her Mother's Shoes

In Belk's   I run fingertips over them—
smooth black calf   laces over the instep
a slight heel: a lady's boot   reminiscent
of the 1890s: not my usual style—
more to your   my daughter's   taste.   I flash you
at home as I last saw you   your fat baby
a diaper over your shoulder   one hand
setting the bottle in the microwave
I had been telling you how   back then   we
had to boil them   & the diapers   too…
And yes   I think I'll have them   the granny shoes
 but in a size larger   an eight   to wear
with thick socks when the winds blow across
the Western plains   on those days when my heart
feels iced even under a quilted vest.
At dawn   the phone rings near my ear   I hear
you strangle out the words   the disbelief
between your sobs: "Mama!… My baby!… He died.!"
& now I know   why I bought the black shoes
in your size   that this time   you will walk
in my shoes   a woman in black   grieving
her child   & there will be no way   Oh God
no way!   that I can walk in yours on this
the day that your life as a woman begins.

Resurrección

Good Friday: I remember
how   at nine   you would lose
your coin purse   how I would walk
down the street   finding at my
feet what was yours   how
you had raced on ahead   already
trusting the kindness of strangers…
And now   before rushing down
a runway   you hand me red
tulips stuck into green glass
(a bottle of orange soda
the only thing you had you said)
And I know how   in two days
in a vase   a kitchen   I will
look into these arms   opening
red & glossy   as bright as
fresh-spilled blood   hearts small
spiked crowns of gold.   And wonder:
will I see you alive again?
Will you too rise from the dead?

Bliss

"Have you really understood how many opportunities you have had to gladden yourself, and how many of them you have refused." —*A Course in Miracles*

You tell me of the can of yellow paint
you threw against the door at the crack dealer
in the by-the-week hotel   the one
with the smell of cat piss down the hall
the carpet a cockroach crust.   Skinny
too beautiful   your hair a wine-red swamp
your blouse a shiny hooker's garb   you tell
me this looking at me with your one
sky-blue eye   the other still brown   a lost
contact   you say   And I recall the Siamese
cat   I saw once on the Bowery
irises just that azure   wall-eyed
ears flattened against further pain.

           And how
when you were nine   the Welch's Grape Juice spread
purple on the cream-colored carpet
how we watched it   not even trying
to get up the spill. "It's so pretty"
you murmured then. And isn't even this brute
gloss   glistening down hollow wood
the bright ochre blood of your rage   as
lovely as the small threads in the eyeball
burst in stroke   as foreign   as chemical

as the rake of a string of knots pulled through
a vein   one by one?   And doesn't that same red
flow through your veins   the crack dealer's   mine
richer   slicker than a red bird's flash   or
strawberries glistening in a silver bowl?
No.   This loveliness does not bring peace.
But can we   even now   note this beauty?
Can rapture blaze where even this pain is?

> *A shock of pure cobalt*
> *in the yard   a bird amid*
> *the cool green spears   the purple*
> *flowers some call weeds.   And*
> *what if I had not looked up*
> *from The Times   my usual*
> *fear   to glance through a glass*
> *to see such blue   such bliss?*

Faith

When the leg with its broken places
was cradled in the cast— white   dense
& thick as crust   I had faith in my
small bones   their fusing: all I had
to do was lie back & wait.   But then
with the buzz of a saw that does not cut
through flesh (they say) that wall fell away
in great chunks   like the scabs from my back
at age six after the boiling spill from
the coffee pot left me a raw chrysalis...

And now this red-haired therapist
an amazon worthy of the SS   rubs
thumbs like steel along the line of red-hot
a brand held to flesh still rosy   as puffy
as a string of small red balloons   as shirred
as shiny as the polished cotton from which
I sewed dresses back in the '50s...

"Walk" she commands   & I do   stumbling
as I must have done at one   yet without
that babe's smile of hope— the faith I held
in the wheelchair   even leaning on a crutch
fallen away like a thin nightgown...
And this is what I am losing again
as you   my daughter insist that South

of the Border   you will use only
the brown stuff   raw & elemental
& yes   just pure enough to help you
withdraw from the Xanax   the methadone.
That within six months   you will return
-- not in a scrawl smuggled from a jail
in south Mexico   not disappeared
or murdered by bandits   the liquid vowels
falling like stars around your wine-red
hair.   Nor leaning on a cane (a nail still
through one ankle   a woman crucified)
will I bring your casket back: no
you insist: this time   you will return
to me risen like an angel   as strong
in the broken places as this young
amazon promises my ankle will be.
And where is my faith this time you ask.

Doctor Landa's Voice

is balm to a fevered
brain   the liquid syllables drifting up
from Guadalajara   a place with gardens—
the Sanatorio San Juan de Dios
the hospital of God...   "Everything
is beautiful here"   you murmur via
long distance.   I see you walking with him
in this movie set   behind you   among
the topiary   the nuns drift like swans
or saints.   You tell him of your mother's rage
your father's lust.   Of your brother   carrying
knives.   Of how you started the hard stuff at twelve
gave one baby up & another died...
And I think how it was for you in Los
Estadas de Unidos: the doctor-gods
their jokes at your expense   the dealers lounging
against store fronts   not to speak of the rapes
the beatings.   Of you   once lovely   in line
with the others at the methadone clinic...
Yes   I think how New York   the cities
of the Deep South became your Beirut   your Bosnia
of how this moment is your first peaceful one
in how many years? And is there a chance—
just a small chance— that you will be spared?
Yet isn't it I who yearn to be held
in the arms of San Juan de Dios

within the comfort of nuns   within
the narrow beds   the taut white cotton
within the walkways lined with flowers—
I who want the chocolate lukewarm
I who want the fruta de plata   bright
at morning   I who want to bend my knees
to hope   I who want to be saved at last…

Portrait of Lily

"I will look to the hills from whence cometh my help."

In Wyoming   I see the far away hills
blue hazed   soft focus   on the side
of the farther one   your portrait hangs:
huge   framed by the gold-backed clouds—
the same photo of you that gazes at me
from atop the frail wicker table   with its
frayed cobalt Guatemalan covering
its stacks of art books & small objects
the sculpture of a woman   crucified—
from which you pierce me with your deep
lashed eyes   your look of tender yearning
as I sit on the yellow couch in my living
room in Savannah: the face of a woman
who is also my daughter   who has also
known grief   a woman whose pain I feel
as though it is mine.   But here   as I look
toward the hills   I see you on the side
of a mountain: as distant   as self-contained
& as beautiful as Mary   or the stars.
And at last   mortal rage: at what was taken
from your life.   What was taken from mine.

Part Two

Without a Mother's Love

"A man cannot die without a mother's love."
—Sigmund Freud

"First-person narrators can't die, so as long as we keep telling the story of our own lives we're safe.   Ha bloody fucking Ha!"
—Pat Barker, Ghost Road

The throw of the dice: two born to dark, one born to light

For Jesús, Eyes Blazing

"I am building my boat, and I will leave in 90 days." —my son David's
diary at age nine

Vengeance is mine, sayeth the Lord.
But you   Jesús   take it on yourself --
vengeance for Maria's death
vengeance for the lost tools
vengeance for your good name
vengeance for your cat   Tunes
& for Charlie Brown   the Abyssinian
left behind when your parents moved.
For your lost Tarzan books
for your grandfather's golf clubs
left rusting out by the garage
for the horses you never rode
except in your dreams…
For the loss of innocence in that detention center
for the loss of sanity with that first hit of speed
the dopamine flooding your brain like a wild fire. . .
Vengeance is mine   sayeth Jesús.
And will the still lake of peace   of happiness
ever fill your mind again   my son?
Unknown to you   you have such
a grandeur about you—standing there

toothless & raging   in jeans full
of holes   old tee shirt & kerchief—
you are due for a miracle   &
you don't even know or want it...

Endangered Species

"Think of him as you would a tiger— beautiful, but you wouldn't want
to get too close."— a social worker just after my son was diagnosed
with paranoid schizophrenia

"Love a wild animal to protect the wild mind inside yourself."—Sam
Keene

The lynx stares out of yellow eyes
from a calendar covered in cellophane
inside a store of many aisles
of disembodied voices like God's—
no vines   no trees here   nothing to hide behind
only the stacks and stacks of things—
sleek   impenetrable   as remote as your mind...

My son   I would have wrapped you thus—
freed from alertness to every rustle
of branch & leaf   from the need for claw
& fang   for yellowed breath.   Instead   I give you

this photo of your tumultuous self
this portrait of the one you were born to be—
this totem animal deep inside your brain
this you   clawing to get out from behind
the deep dark eyes   the glassy gaze
of your elemental & perfect madness.

Some cats   the more beautiful

& dangerous ones— the jaguar
the leopard   the tiger— because
of the construction of their throats
cannot purr. Could it be   my son
that you are merely one of these?

The Rules

"People have died for what is in this bag."— my son of the plastic bag
he carries everywhere

---

double locks on the doors
standing guard always
the personal spoken only in whispers—
no light let in   even on the 14th floor—

else they might watch us by telescope.
And what of your lover's murderers?

On your old upright Royal
you record everything:
minute by minute   the messages they send.

They live in the apartment above.
They call your name through the heat registers.
And the lock on your file cabinet?   Broken again.
There are spies everywhere—
the man who comes to fix the thermostat…

And why, you spew an inch from my face
can't you understand: That you must be
vigilant.   That they will kill you, too?

The arm I once cradled   dimpled & plump
now hovers above me   hard   brown   muscular—

your black eyes blaze   you rage in the thrall
of what you know to be true.   I listen.   And yes
I am afraid: Of you.   For you, my son…

How Dumb Can You Be

*for Betty Shabazz, Malcolm X's widow, who died at 61 with third degree
burns over 80 percent of her body*

"But what he did was so awful," —a friend, of John Salvi's murder of
the abortion clinic nurses

---

to stand there in your fast-melting flesh—
"smoldering," the papers said— and cry
"what will become of my grandson?"
the 12-year-old who made you thus
the boy you asked to save from the daughter
who had already tortured you for years?
As dumb as the preacher who goes to his
mad son's house   an unlikely pistol
in his coat pocket   hoping to convince
& heal   only to be knifed to death?
Like the suburban mom   nailed into
a closet by her own boy   who   a few days
later will hack her & his dad to death?
As dumb as the Salvis   thinking it's not that bad
that a lot of kids have a hard time adjusting
that maybe some   like their John   hear blackbirds
speaking… And how dumb am I   trying
to save you?   But this is not intellect or smarts
this is etched into the brain   filaments   wires
running deeper than the need to flee:
the small animal   defending her young

against eyes bright & yellow   against tooth
& claw   a beast relentless   bigger than
we are   always. Always   waiting to spring…

The Murderous Sky

With bloodied breasts   Magritte's
birds fly upside down   amid
rocks   against just such cobalt
a sky as killing as this one.
Yet this is not crazed canvas
the outback or a veld   but
Exit 68   off I-95   South
Florida   Fahrenheit 106...

Yes   this is Amerika
land of the Golden Arches
of Waffle Houses   of melting
margarine   of time shares sold
over glittery formica
of Corvettes   Camaros   blazing
like comets down ribbons
of asphalt. Where I too speed
The Book of Virtues spinning
on CD   the miles silver
beneath my wheels. And here
into this land of the sun
come these two wretched ones—
burnt flesh served up on the plate
of the dry earth. One staggers
barefoot   curls matted   skin
smeared as black as an aborigine's

up the embankment.   And then
his companion in this hell:
too brown   too thin   half-clothed
bent over a piece of cardboard…
And all I can think is,
what if one of them had
been you? Dear God, what
if one of them had been you?

And Isn't It Ironic

for Carmen, who grew up in Georgia in two rooms off a railway
station where her father was stationmaster, who, as a young wife and
mother, ran away to Arizona, and became a nurse, an alcoholic and a
paraplegic, who spent 25 years of her life in a wheelchair, the last five
of them cared for my schizophrenic son David

that the very fiery stuff

that was in you when you swerved

off that road in Arizona

to wake in a gully of sand

feeling nothing from the waist down—

the very booze that traveled

your bloodstream   even as you lay

paralyzed for those first moments

that would turn into a lifetime

in a wheelchair   cursing & striking

out with your Helping Hand

or else   for a long time   still

tempting men with the sparkle

of your black eyes...   Oh   for a time

you tried things to while away

what life you had: the taxidermy

the contests in which you won beach bags—

making your own beef jerky

in a dehydrator   Black men

in the deep South & scandalizing

the neighbors   writing poetry

in truck stops   & always   chaos...

Yes   isn't it ironic that
the very stuff you used
up to the end to bear the pain
of what you had done to yourself
with it   leads you now to lie
breathless   a fat nurse whispering
to let go   let Jesus   the poisoned
fluid around your rotting liver
squeezing tight   kidney stones like
quarters passing from your dead
urethra   flesh like beefsteak bleeding
onto the bed sheet (but of course
you could feel nothing of that) in this
white hospital bed   dying at last.

Confirmed Negativity

"Illusion— it's the very air they breathe!"— The old magician, *Summer and Smoke*, by Woody Allen

---

"Confirmed negativity… a failure to thrive"
the expert says of you   the big-eyed
three-year-old sitting on her lap: you
who by choice live on 20 Cheerios a day…
who knew from your first months that life
was too difficult to try.   Yet   sweet boy
how did you know so soon that everything
that happens will be worse than we thought:
how dangerous life is   & how much pain?

Or is your god like this physical therapist
who leads me   my leg swathed in white
just carved & stitched   to the edge of a steep
stair well to practice how to move three steps
up   three steps down: a boy insisting I ignore
the possible shattering   the excruciation
of what can happen   what probably will?

Yes   what is the difference in you   child
& we who casually (or not so casually)
shed the knowledge of boys with box cutters
in hand   thumbs at the ready   of men
fattening on what rots our cells   of our
own kind   chewing on cardboard   freezing
under bridges?   What trick   what delusion
makes us this unwise?   What makes you so sane?

Carpal Tunnel

It's all in the wrist:
to change the diaper
to reach out the hand
to beat the eggs   to set the table
to wipe away the blood
to bind the wound
to bring the bed tray
to take the bed pan
to smooth the brow
to pick up the telephone
to write out the money order
to tap out the message
to wrest the shotgun
to write the truth
to copy the forbidden book
to hide the hunted—
it's all in the wrist
a twist that moves outward…

But what if one does not?
The wrist is caught
in a forward motion
bound there forever
as though by invisible wires…

Some of us think we can avoid

this disease. By accusing—
"Why didn't you leave?"…
"Why did you do that?"…
"Why did you let him?"…
Why didn't…? Why did…?
Why didn't…? Why did…?
By staying still.   By looking
the other way. Some of us
are wrong: tendons shrink
we shrivel   grow claws
hands that would not   cannot:

a crippling of the heart
a hardening of everything—
all grief goes inward.

So let it be. Look. Feel   Do.
It's all in the wrist. *Love is.*

Things Falling, or Why the Beautiful Die Young

for Barry, who dreamed in the days and nights before he died of China,
where he had never been

"I feel odd."— Alexander Graham Bell's father's last words

Lately I've seen things falling—
cellophane packages   vanilla
wafers   off a grocery table—
fur coats from a chair in a house
with track lights   faux columns.
Before that   it was my son into
madness   the state   my daughter
into white powder   the softness
of needles   a friend into AIDS—
that death that comes too soon. And
now you   love   into drink & regret…

And each time there is that moment
when I imagine I can reach out
my hand   hold back the cookies
the coats   my loved ones   that I can
save them by the strength of my wrist
the twist of it   even near breaking…

Instead   I feel my own frailty—
the stick held out over quicksand
or the mother's arm gone numb

in the cattle car in those
movies we all saw as kids—

& I know that I must let you drop
that I will be left holding nothing
but the frail rag of my love
clutching   like the woman in
Syria   the felt cowboy hat
the boy-child left   a remnant
of my daughter's dress   my friend's
paintings   the ones before he got
famous   your papers for a foreign
legion: that I will clasp these

against that night when I cannot
stay my own slide into what must
be like that first hit of dope   or
falling through that hole into China—
into that vast & billowy comforter
(as sweet   as warming   as hot chocolate)
into which we each slip like newborns

when you   by the strength of your wrist
pull me down into the inevitable
burnout   that charcoal falling to ash
that dark   now gentle   companionable.

Squeezing the Cat

"Damn! He's good looking!"
My son   the guitar player
holds the audience enthralled
in this little bar where a dozen
women hang on to his every note.
Or even a huge hall   some vast space
with those far away in the bleachers
barely able to see him—
a hush falls   then the yells
as he comes forth.   Then afterwards
those who rush forth to touch him…
this son who has loved guitars
from the moment he held one
in those bad boy bands…

But instead   it was first drugs
the dealers with shotguns   with chains
the strange utterances the threats.
Then carrying everything you own
in a black plastic garbage bag
and me mailing you boxes of food—
"Don't give him cash," my therapist says.
And the visit with my daughter
when you hold us hostage
play every song you've written.
And at last the diagnosis

paranoid schizophrenia
(hospitals   disability   the right meds at last).

But still the guitar in your hand
the words you sing
your one constant.
And then comes the other:
the terminal cancer.
And again   it's your guitar
that you depend on
and drugs & hopeless little bands
misfits like you at the apartment building for the disabled
hitting me up for bucks for musical equipment.
At the end   you're still trying to start a real band.
And after the chemo   the radiation
you even pick up a new woman
travel with her to Jacksonville.
"Mother, I don't have any natural urges anymore,"
you say when you come back.
"Cocaine in his blood work," the doctor says
in the E.R. a few weeks later
where you're taken
struggling for breath.

And then it's over:
And I'm left with the musical scores in your hand
(yes   brilliant in places)
and the small plastic cassette
"Squeezing the Cat, and Other Songs."

Out West, Where I Took My Grief

"We are all H, I.V. Positive." — tattoo on the left hand of vocalist and
performance artist Dimanda Galás

1.

What Keith the rancher said about castrating the bulls:
"We wear a rubber glove   up over the elbow—
the calves   they're held up there with 'em hangin' down
we pull 'em out   till the blood vessels break: that way
they heal up quick   don't bleed so much.   We just cut 'em off
toss 'em into a bucket.   They're good sliced up   fried
with a little batter on 'em.   Once I kept throwing 'em into
one a those rubber gloves   then threw it into the freezer—
some woman saw it 'n started screamin'   thinkin'
it was somebody's amputated arm in there…
Does it hurt the bulls like it would a man?   You bet!
They've got the same nerve endin's.   But there's a difference:
for them   it's just that one second: they don't think
about it 'fore hand   they don't think about it afterwards… "

And yes   as children   didn't we each dream it would be
different for us?   That we would somehow escape
unscathed?   I read somewhere that suffering is not
the pain itself   but staying in the pain.   And
that's what we humans are good at.   Memory
that blessing & curse   makes it easy to grieve
for a lifetime   to think of what was & what might
have been.   While the cattle stand knee-deep in snow

or lie among the rocks   rough brush   dreamless
we toss in warm beds   knowing   too well what the next
phone call   the next day might bring: that each moment
of peace   holds within it   a hidden twin: the teratoma
of our missing parts: the seeds of our loss   or of someone's.

2.

Keith the rancher tells how the calves become steers:
"… Or if they're young calves   we just rope 'em
We take 'em back to their mamas a couple of weeks
to get healed up from the cuttin'   the brandin'—
let'em have some milk   get 'em on the grain…
Then when they're yearlin's or short yearlin's
we ship 'em out as feeders to Sheridan or some
where   crowd 'em in there 'bout two thousand
to an acre… It ust to be that we waited longer
to build up more muscle 'n all. But now
that we can inject 'em with the hormones…
Do they cry when they're taken?   You bet—
the calves holler for a couple a days. And their
mamas beller.   But that's just instinct   the way
it is."   *And besides who but we are their gods?*

3.

What Keith the hunter says
about the deer in the hills:
"During the huntin'
season   it's the young

ones   that get hit
the old bucks know
to stay put.   Once
I shot a doe   she kept
runnin' every time
she had a chance   she'd
lie down   lick 'erself—
it was the adrenalin
that saved 'er. That 'n
the saliva— there's
somethin' healin'
in it.   Like tears."

In Massachusetts

I am packed in ice   the bleeding
of my severed limb stopped   held
in a blanket of soft gray   turned
fuzzy by pale street lights.
Even the cold seems warm here.
For a long time— a decade? two?
happiness has escaped me.   And
the amputation of which I speak?
At first   I assumed it to be
a mother gone to suicide
a father lost to booze   a daughter
turned to junk & the streets
a once-handsome son   his mind
blown   taken in handcuffs.   Or
the small things: the husbands dropped
like pennies along the way...

But no: what was lost was
the house with the goldfish pond
the beds full of tangled sheets
stamped with bright jungle creatures
the rooms warmed by the glow
of kids   apricot-hipped   rosy
from their baths   racing the
yellow-lit spaces   the daffodils
bunched in a jar   the red cat

twisting at my ankle   the steam
from the just-cooked dishes
the gold of a lemon meringue pie
beaded with crystals of sugar—
this was what was lost to the black
hole (the nausea   the churning
of it): the chunks of me   the froth—
the acrylic fluff of halcyon days…

So I am happy to be here in
Massachusetts   wrapped in this
dull gray blanket   packed in ice
like white sound   muffled between
gray rock & bare trees: grateful
for the crunch of snow beneath
my boots   a buffer for all that
has happened   content to watch
from afar   a bundled figure
skating on a pond   as graceful
as a distant saint   to know
that I'm a thousand miles from
Georgia   that here   my blood
coagulates to a mere freeze

else it might spill like a fish
in a seafood counter   leaking
red through white numbness   darkening
the thick gray ice with the grief
of what I have lost of myself.

Part Three

Beautiful Things

"There is no beauty without my beast."— Stevie Nicks

"Perhaps everything terrible is, in its deepest being, something helpless that wants help from us."— Maria Ranier Rilke, *Letters to a Young Poet*

"One does not become enlightened by imagining figures of light, but by making the darkness conscious." – Carl Jung

Values, or the Christ of the White Shag Carpet

"The man in the violent situation reveals those qualities least dispensable in his personality, those qualities which are all he will have to take into eternity with him."—Flannery O'Connor

---

The boy in Kansas— or was it Nebraska?
whose two arms were pulled off by the farm machine
jerked from their very sockets   walked some distance through
　　the fields
just how far was it?   into the empty house
dialed the phone   *how?   with his nose?*
then stood in the bathtub until the ambulance came
so not to get blood on his mothers wall-to-wall shag
Later   his arms were reattached   which goes to show
how   *if every American boy had values like these*
no old ladies would be disemboweled with a poker
by a youth who only smirked when questioned
no three-year-old would have her liver ruptured
by the man her mother takes into her bed...

No   none of this would happen if we all lived
in Nebraska & did the right thing   if we all
had more of those all-American values.
And the moral of this story is: don't bleed
onto the carpet   that perfect cream acrylic
that virtuous & unmarked   that wall-to-wall
white shag   that our mothers lived & suffered
& died for.   And above all   don't cry out

86

& then   & only then   will your original
wound be healed   your arm   if not your heart   replaced
into its gaping hole.   But one last word   please:
don't believe this   don't believe any of this.

The Power of Love

"I love them as poets love the poetry that kills them, as drowned sailors
love the sea."—Derek Walcott

The boy is clawing his burning sister
from the burning sports car (a Triumph   I think)—
she's stuck & he's shouting   *I love you!*
& she's shouting it back   & they're both screaming.
But the power of love can't save her—
he socks the cop who drags him away.
And for the rest of his life he lives
with that guilt: as a young man lying
on beaches   in strange beds   as a father
looking into the face of his baby daughter
at thirty   slurring to the barkeep
"another double"   pouring into his flesh
what he dreams will put out memory.
"Oh   stop blubbering," the woman with him
sulls   not caring about how he failed   how
if he had been a *real* man   & doesn't
he know people don't want to *hear* about that!?
Still   on his death bed at fifty   the slime
of cancer filling his lungs   his last vision
as *drowning   drowning*   he goes under is
his sister going up in flames   & what
he hears are her screams: *I love you! I love you!*
& they're both crying & screaming
of how the power of love can't save her

of how the power of love can't save him…
This is what the boy hears on his deathbed
& I think how the power of my love can't save
you or anyone   of how   no matter
how hard I tug   I can't pull you from the blaze
of madness   of drugs   of disease.   & how
like that boy   his sister   you too will reach
out your arms   you too will pull me close
to the flames   screaming   *I love you!   I love you!*
How I too will die hearing your cries.

Portrait: Boy With Dog

after *The Scream* by Edvard Munch

"Hereditary mange"
you tell me in the vet's
waiting room.   I look
away   from the oozing
skin   the bleeding toes --
"He's three months old --
I've been working over-
time at Burger King
to bring him here."   I thought
he was an old dog --
older than you who
look twenty   who could
be out loving girls
& good times   your jet
eyes as lush-lashed   as
sexy as Elvis's   your
thick brows drawn by
by Michelangelo   age
before my eyes   your
dark face spoiled by
a few patches of bad
skin   early pain &
grief   already trapped
by your need to keep

alive this useless beast.
"Have you had him
tested for heart worms?"
the clerk calls out   "It
may not make sense to
keep him going. . . "   I see
the horror in your eyes
the horror of the mother
at the son's death sentence
as the word AIDS drips
from her daughter's lips.
And I know that you   too
must do this: work over-
time at Burger King
writhe   pleasureless   in
your narrow bed   wake
each morning to this sick
beast   bleeding   dying
at eye level   a gaze
as pleading as yours is.
And that it is this: this
animal love that drives
you   that this   my raw
beautiful Christ   *is*
what your life means.

Intimate Terrorists

Last week a military court in Peru sentenced (Lori) Berenson, 26, to life
in prison for treason…Police say she helped supply arms, a safe house
and intelligence information to the Marxist Tupac Amaru revolutionary
movement…"—*Newsweek*, January 22, 1996

"She moved to Peru as an idealistic young woman hoping to change
the world, only to be thrown into prison for abetting antigovernment
rebels. Fifteen years later, she is finally out of captivity, a single
mother struggling to figure out what comes next." —*New York Times
Magazine*, March 6, 2011

"…the universe seems decent because decent people have gelded eyes."
—George Bataille, *Story of the Eye*

"I can't sit back and watch TV
while people are starving," you said
to your dad   an American college
professor. "I told her to follow
her heart," he   grieving   says now.
Yes   Lori   you were raised right—
one of those good liberal kids
born to a do-gooder strain   full
of the desire to do the right thing…
And who among us could resist
that great bonus thrown in   the lure
of the jungle   Indiana Jones
South of the Border & all that?
Once   it was Eva Marie Saint
sleeping with a young Paul Newman
fighting for Israel   even

if she *was* blonde   a shiksa…
And probably some cute Marxist
his big baby browns   muscular
thighs   appealed to *every*thing:
your groin   your desire to help
& help…   "There's not one terrorist
among them!"   you screech from the photo
in *Newsweek*   an average-pretty
girl in blue jeans flanked by two
unsmiling guards   women in dark
glasses   high heels   double-breasted
suits   oozing the kind of cruel
glamour filling third world movies…
Yet the state department (the state
department?)   says you're deluded
that there is proof: of robberies
bombings   assassinations.   And
here you are   about to be thrown
into prison for life: *Yanamayo…*
where inmates have their food
their daylight   rationed…   Lori
have you   with your good girl's heart
been as conned as I have by those
I hold dear   the strung out   the insane
the clever ones who daily convince
me that they only live through my
blood sacrifice?   Are their garbled
cries as much a plant as your hand-

writing   scribbled over diagrams
drawings of weapons   left to be found
in your Lima apartment? And
will my liberal heart and yours
continue to bleed & bleed (not
to speak of your sweet parents')
while those who learned early to look
away   eyes blinkered   to keep
noses clean   enjoy what you & I
were born to   but can't quite? Or
a half-century from now   shaped
to that rock   a woman long shriveled
will you look back   scoff at the love
the beliefs   yes   the very kindnesses
that took away *everything?*

Poverty

"…Like the disregarded ones we turned against
because we'd failed them by our disregard."
—Seamus Heaney

---

is no art: there is no art in it—
no roses full blown in a crystal vase
no paintings casually stacked against a wall
no photos of loved ones in silver frames
no scent of cilantro   saffron   wafting
from a kitchen   no lotions no massages
no trips to the seaside   no hardcover books
no laughing with friends in a bistro
discussing the film…

instead   the smell of cat piss
the crack dealer across the hall   the one
small meal a day at a place filled with those
like yourself   & the memory of another time
sloshing vague in your brain   when   with your
mother and father   you went to New York
City   to museums   to restaurants—
in China Town   they laughed that you wanted
to be a psychiatrist who lived on a farm
or a painter   better even than Picasso…
But that was long ago   before you can even
recall   And now you have dirt & rage
& when you luck up   a hit of dope. For
poverty is no art.   There is no art in it.

Daytona Raceway

The woman in a cheap print dress, a slight hump at her back
styleless gray scraggles of hair, asks the Day's Inn clerk
for a room for another night: "Why do we have to check out
now?" Her son, graying, fiftyish, stands back, head bent.
"We'll see what we can do," the clerk, an Indian, says,
"but at the moment we're booked up." "Where's the bus stop?"
she asks. The Indian points through the glass to an already
blazing South Florida morning, across the four-lane that leads
onto the interstate. "See that pole over there? That's it."
After I pay, I get into my Camaro, scanning the dazzling
roadway, the vast asphalt, but they have gone. Why do I
always have to see such as them? Or the Black man—gray face,
gray shirt, gray pants -- leaning back as if stunned on thin
elbows at the freeway exit. Or the skinny one I will
glimpse tonight. rain-soaked, looking lost, holding one small
suitcase, on my way to the restaurant with my husband
where amid the white cloths, the low lights, the golden loaves,
the dish of oil, its island of cheese; the vodka martinis (extra
olives, extra large) I must not think of them. . . No, I must
not think of them. For who are they to me? *Everything*.

Luck

for Lorraine

"When will my luck change?"—ad for a telephone psychic

You called today to say that two years ago
your second daughter Kathleen was beaten
to death with a sledge hammer   that last year
your third daughter Jill ran off with the drugs   that
her dealer threatened your life   & you
wrote him a check for all your small savings:
that luckily   he was murdered before
he came back the next week: all this a few years
after your first daughter   Lori   shot you
in the head   & then shot herself...
        But
the up side of this   you say   is that
you've separated from the husband
who blamed it on menopause when you dyed
your hair blonde   had your face lifted   went out
dancing   found a younger boyfriend   thus
he claimed   inciting Lori's mother-killing
rage. As you talk   I recall a dozen
years ago: you   a small graying woman as
impressionless as a nickel   asking me
the published author to speak at your church
of how the next time we met   you lifted
a Clairoled strand to show the scars still raging

behind an ear (you had offered a gift
a bunch of azaleas   you said   instead
Lori had raised the pistol   and when
she ran out of bullets   drove off to buy more
giving you time to drag yourself   bleeding
down a stair).   For one moment   as you talked
your golden hair glowed   a halo.   And I think
now how we are sisters   yes   how pain guts
& levels us…   Oh   I know some would say
there must be something wrong with you   that not
so much could come to one innocent woman.
But I know otherwise: how the fates can load
the dice & throw them in one direction.   *Ours*.

Beautiful Things

are often dangerous: the silver plane
(single-engine, bullet hole in fuselage)
all that holds us up over the jungle—
cloud beneath   a mattress   a featherbed
the orange & black tiger padding below
the coral & lemon snakes dripping   face-
level   alligators gliding the swamps
(eyes like small yellow headlights)   *a child's*
bedtime toys   primary colors.   And
handling the rattlers is shiver   is tickle
is jump rope to Washed in the Blood.   And what
of the charcoal sky just before hurricane
the snow that collapses to avalanche?   And
oh!   those tender peaks of the Tetons
crevices drawing our fingers like mittens—
walking into white-out: to freeze   it's said
is fugue state   is bliss   is the perfect death...
And needles full of morphine & morphine
dreams   & sex with beautiful strangers
& standing on drug streets at 3 a.m... .
All this comes after the loves like injections
of Drano   after we   weary novitiates
have been brought to our knees.   For this is
the happiness of the insane   of we who
have left behind clocks   lawns   meals at six:
it is as though the brain has been razed

our words rip forth   scalpels dripping red.
And now we come to that edge   that first
slice at the wrist (exquisite   glacial)
that razor that will delight or kill: yes
dangerous things are often beautiful
blinding us to the fangs   the needles
the peaks   that will throw us off-center
to the dogs   but still   we keep testing
that edge   until we are nothing but pain
even the dope can't fix   until we are
bloodied   in ribbons   scattered   until
we are at last restitched & remade —
rearranged so that we turn from it.
Yet always it is that edge that we grieve.

April in Massachusetts

"I cannot believe that the inscrutable universe turns on an axis of suffering; surely the strange beauty of the world must somehow rest on pure joy."—Louise Bogan

"Before Wordsworth, daffodils were called weeds."— Rebecca West

---

a few yellow buds

& two full-blown purple crocuses

with butter centers

right where the ice was last week—

after years of too many azaleas

(frantic   blood-flushed)

this suddenly is enough.

Wyoming

"There is only one important question: is the universe friendly?" —
Albert Einstein on his death bed

What do we learn from the inexorable landscape?
Only what the animals have always known—
that we are frail. And that we are not God.

Stigmata

always bursts from the palms.
While the actual nails
were driven through His forearms.
And how much of our joy
our pain is illusion?

Halleluiah!   And yes
miracles do happen.
You are reborn   as
it's said   is He.

ROSEMARY DANIELL'S collections of poetry include *A Sexual Tour of the Deep South* (Holt, Rinehart & Winston; Push Button Publishing) and *Fort Bragg & Other Points South* (Henry Holt & Company); a chapbook, *The Feathered Trees*, was edited by Georgia Poet Laureate David Bottoms and published by Sweetwater Press. Her recently completed memoir is *My Beautiful Tigers: Forty Years as the Mother of an Opioid Addicted Daughter and a Schizophrenic Son.* Her book, *Secrets of the Zona Rosa: How Writing (and Sisterhood) Can Change Women's Lives*, was published by Henry Holt and Company. Its prequel, *The Woman Who Spilled Words All Over Herself: Writing and Living the Zona Rosa Way*, was published by Faber & Faber. Her memoir, *Fatal Flowers: On Sin, Sex and Suicide in the Deep South* (Holt, Rinehart & Winston; Henry Holt & Company; Hill Street Press) won the 1999 Palimpsest Prize for a most-requested out-of-print book, and was re-issued that same year. Along with her second memoir, *Sleeping with Soldiers* (Holt, Rinehart & Winston; Hill Street Press), which was also published as part of the Book of the Month Club's Library of Erotic Classics, it was a forerunner of the current memoir trend. Her other books include a collection of essays, *Confessions of a (Female) Chauvinist* (Hill Street Press), and a novel, *The Hurricane Season* (William Morrow & Company). Among her awards are two N.E.A. Fellowships in creative writing, one in poetry, another in fiction, as well as the William Wisdom-William Faulkner gold medal in poetry. In addition to her many publications in literary magazines, her features and reviews have appeared in numerous magazines and papers, including *Harper's Bazaar, New York Woman, Mademoiselle, The New York Times Book Review* and *Mother Jones*; she has also been a guest on many national radio and television shows, such as Merve Griffin, Donahue, The Diane Rehm Show, Larry King Live and CNN's "Portrait of America." She is profiled in the book *Feminists Who Changed America, 1963-1975*. In 2008, she received a Governor's Award in the Humanities for her impact on the state of Georgia; early in her career, she instigated and led writing workshops in women's prisons in Georgia and Wyoming, served as program director for Georgia's Poetry in the Schools, and worked for a dozen years in Poetry in the Schools programs in Georgia, South Carolina, and Wyoming. Also known as one of the best writing coaches in the country, she is the founder and leader of Zona Rosa, a series of creative writing workshops in Savannah and Atlanta, and cities throughout the world, as described in People and Southern Living magazines, and attended by such outstanding authors as John Berendt, Bruce Feiler and Pat Conroy. To date, almost 300 Zona Rosans and counting have become published authors.

Lavender Ink
lavenderink.org